FROM SEA to SHINING SEA

TENNESSEE

MYRA S. WEATHERLY

Consultants

MELISSA N. MATUSEVICH, PH.D.

Curriculum and Instruction Specialist
Blacksburg, Virginia

LISA HOOVER

Director of Children's Services
La Vergne Public Library
La Vergne, Tennessee

CHILDREN'S PRESS®

A DIVISION OF SCHOLASTIC INC.

New York • Toronto • London • Auckland • Sydney • Mexico City
New Delhi • Hong Kong • Danbury, Connecticut

Tennessee is located in the Southern region of the United States. Other states in this region are Alabama, Arkansas, Delaware, Florida, Georgia, Kentucky, Louisiana, Maryland, Mississippi, North Carolina, South Carolina, Virginia, and West Virginia.

Project Editor: Lewis K. Parker
Art Director: Marie O'Neill
Photo Researcher: Marybeth Kavanagh
Design: Robin West, Ox and Company, Inc.
Page 6 map and recipe art: Susan Hunt Yule
All other maps: XNR Productions, Inc.

Library of Congress Cataloging-in-Publication Data

Weatherly, Myra.
    Tennessee/ Myra S. Weatherly.
        p. cm.—(From sea to shining sea)
    Includes bibliographical references and index.
    ISBN 0-516-22312-7
    1. Tennessee—Juvenile literature. [1. Tennessee.] I. Title. II. From sea to shining sea (Series)
F436.3 .W43 2001
976.8—dc21   00-065943

TABLE of CONTENTS

CHAPTER

ONE   Introducing the Volunteer State 4

TWO   The Land of Tennessee 7

THREE   Tennessee Through History 15

FOUR   Governing Tennessee 43

FIVE   The People and Places of Tennessee 52

Tennessee Almanac 70

Timeline 72

Gallery of Famous Tennesseans 74

Glossary 75

For More Information 76

Index 77

INTRODUCING THE VOLUNTEER STATE

Tennessee offers many adventures, including whitewater rafting.

Tennessee is easy to locate on a map. The state is shaped like a ship plowing its way from the Mississippi River toward the Atlantic Ocean. It is a small state—thirty-five other states are larger.

Tennessee was not one of the original thirteen states. Before becoming a part of the United States, people who lived in eastern Tennessee founded their own state. The independent state was called Franklin, named for Benjamin Franklin. It had its own governor and coined its own money.

When Tennessee became a territory of the United States, it took its name from *Tanasie*, a Cherokee village. Tennessee's nickname, the Volunteer State, comes from the large number of Tennesseans who offered to fight in the War of 1812. Tennessee is also sometimes called the "Big Bend State," which refers to the Indian name of the Tennessee River.

What comes to mind when you think of Tennessee?

- ❖ Frontier people trekking across the Appalachian Mountains
- ❖ People finding underground wonders
- ❖ Country musicians performing at the Grand Ole Opry
- ❖ People boating on the Cumberland River
- ❖ People backpacking in the Great Smokies
- ❖ Visitors enjoying the world's largest freshwater aquarium
- ❖ Tourists riding a powerful roller coaster at Dollywood
- ❖ People lining up to visit Graceland, Elvis Presley's home

Tennessee is home to exciting places, beautiful scenery, and most of all, music! Turn the page to discover the story of Tennessee.

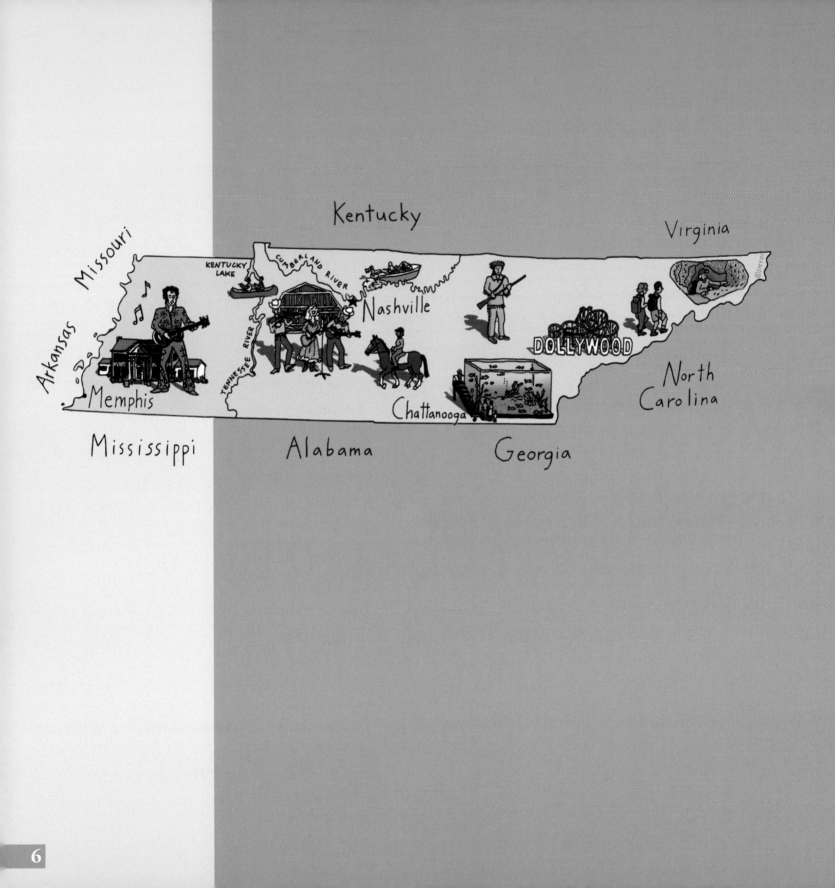

Arkansas

Missouri

Kentucky

Virginia

KENTUCKY LAKE

CUMBERLAND RIVER

TENNESSEE RIVER

Nashville

DOLLYWOOD

North Carolina

Memphis

Chattanooga

Mississippi

Alabama

Georgia

CHAPTER TWO

THE LAND OF TENNESSEE

Tennessee is a long, thin state—it is four times as long as it is wide. Tennessee stretches from the towering Appalachian Mountains to the broad Mississippi River. Its total area is 42,146 square miles (109,158 square kilometers). North Carolina is to the east of Tennessee. Georgia, Alabama, and Mississippi are to the south. Kentucky and Virginia lie to the north. In the west, Arkansas and Missouri border the Volunteer State.

Tennessee's geography is both old and new. The Appalachian Mountains rose from Earth's crust millions of years ago. They are the oldest mountains east of the Mississippi River. In contrast, Reelfoot Lake is young. Reelfoot was created when powerful earthquakes struck northwest Tennessee in the winter of 1811–1812. The earthquakes caused holes in the

In this view, the sun sets over the Cumberland Mountains.

FIND OUT MORE

Ancient people believed that the movement of giant snakes, turtles, or catfish living underneath the ground created earthquakes. What really causes earthquakes? How are earthquakes measured? What do scientists say about the chances of another earthquake happening in Tennessee?

Reelfoot Lake covers 13,000 acres. Bald eagles stay here during the winter months, building nests in the giant cypress trees.

ground. The earthquake also caused the Mississippi River to flow backward, filling the gigantic holes. Reelfoot Lake covers about 13,000 acres (5,261 hectares). It is the largest natural lake in Tennessee.

GEOGRAPHIC REGIONS

Tennessee has three major geographic regions spread over three parts of the state—East Tennessee, Middle Tennessee, and West Tennessee. Because the regions are so different, Tennessee is sometimes thought of as three states in one.

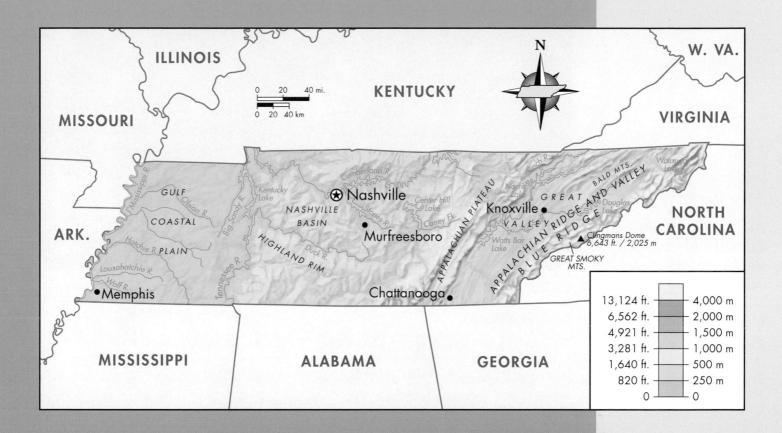

ILLINOIS

KENTUCKY

W. VA.

MISSOURI

VIRGINIA

0   20   40 mi.

0   20   40 km

N

MISSISSIPPI

ALABAMA

GEORGIA

ARK.

NORTH CAROLINA

Memphis

Nashville

Murfreesboro

Knoxville

Chattanooga

Mississippi R.

Obion R.

GULF

COASTAL

PLAIN

Hatchie R.

Loosahatchie R.

Wolf R.

Big Sandy R.

Tennessee R.

Duck R.

Kentucky Lake

Cumberland R.

NASHVILLE BASIN

HIGHLAND RIM

Stones R.

Center Hill Lake

Caney Fk.

APPALACHIAN PLATEAU

Clinch R.

Norris Lake

GREAT VALLEY

APPALACHIAN RIDGE AND VALLEY

BLUE RIDGE

BALD MTS.

Watauga Lake

Douglas Lake

Watts Bar Lake

Clingmans Dome
6,643 ft. / 2,025 m

GREAT SMOKY MTS.

13,124 ft.   4,000 m
6,562 ft.   2,000 m
4,921 ft.   1,500 m
3,281 ft.   1,000 m
1,640 ft.   500 m
820 ft.   250 m
0   0

From Pinnacle Overlook in the Cumberland Gap, you can see parts of seven states.

FIND OUT MORE

The Great Smoky Mountains are named for the bluish haze that hangs over the mountains. What might cause this haze?

East Tennessee

The Appalachian Mountains form Tennessee's easternmost border. The beautiful Great Smoky Mountains is a mountain range in the Appalachians. Black bears are a common sight in these mountains, hiding among the pine trees and mountain laurel.

Tennessee's highest peak, Clingman's Dome, is found in these mountains. Clingman's Dome rises 6,643 feet (2,025 meters). It is the second highest mountain east of the Mississippi River. Only North Carolina's Mount Mitchell at 6,684 feet (2,037 m) is higher. You can see as far as 100 miles (161 km) and parts of seven states from the top of Clingman's Dome.

Wooded mountain ridges and broad valleys are found in East Tennessee. The area is rich in coal, oil, and natural gas. In this region, Fall Creek Falls—the highest waterfall east of the Rocky Mountains—plunges 256 feet (78 m) into a gorge.

Middle Tennessee

In Middle Tennessee, high plains surround a bowl-shaped dip in Earth's surface.

This basin has rich farmland. Cattle, sheep, and the famous Tennessee Walking Horses graze in the pastures. The horses are named for their graceful gait. Tennessee Walking Horses have been bred in the area around Shelbyville and Lynchburg since the late 1700s.

Tennessee Walking Horses graze in a field.

11

The highlands form a brim around the basin. Red cedars grow on the hilly parts. Mineral deposits include limestone, iron, oil, and natural gas. Caves are under much of the land.

Tennessee's caves have been discovered in many ways. For example, more than fifty years ago, two small boys discovered a cave near Knoxville. Because of the lake at the end of the cavern, it is called the Lost Sea. The boys were not the first to explore the cave. Bones and footprints of prehistoric animals were found in a large pit. The skeleton of a giant jaguar found in the cave is now in New York's American Museum of Natural History. Scientists believe the animal may have weighed 500 pounds (227 kilograms).

West Tennessee

West Tennessee is separated from the bordering states by the Mississippi River, and from Middle Tennessee by the Tennessee River. This area is a part of the East Gulf Coastal Plain with rolling hills, wide valleys, and flatlands. Farmers grow cotton and soybeans in the rich soil.

CLIMATE

Tennessee has a mild climate most of the year, except in the mountains. The warmest temperatures occur in the southwest. The coolest temperatures are in the mountain areas. The state's highest recorded temperature was 113° Fahrenheit (45° Celsius) on August 9, 1930 at Perryville. The lowest recorded temperature was -32° F (-36° C) at Mountain

City on December 30, 1917. Tennessee receives a lot of rain. The average precipitation (rainfall and snowfall) is 52 inches (132 centimeters) a year.

This scene shows winter in Kingsport, a city nestled deep in the mountains.

RIVERS

Tennessee's major rivers are the Mississippi River, along the state's western border, and the Tennessee and Cumberland Rivers. The state's longest river is the Tennessee River. It runs 652 miles (1,049 km) between western and central Tennessee. The Tennessee River is formed by the meeting of the French Broad and Holston Rivers east of

Fog settles on the Big South Fork of the Cumberland River.

Knoxville. Flowing southward, it loops through northern Alabama. Then it flows northward across Tennessee again to join the Ohio River in Kentucky. The Cumberland River rises in Kentucky and twists its way through northern Tennessee before reentering Kentucky to join the Ohio.

CHAPTER THREE

TENNESSEE THROUGH HISTORY

Scientists have found fossils in rocks throughout Tennessee. The earliest fossils are the remains of water animals. These fossils tell scientists that millions of years ago the area was covered by warm, shallow seas. After the seas dried up, the land became warm and moist. Plant and dinosaur fossils have been found in the sandstone of West Tennessee.

Thousands of years before humans set foot in present-day Tennessee, thick forests covered the land. Farther north, the land was covered by ice. Large animals traveled southward in search of food. Herds of bison (buffalo), mammoths, and mastodons once roamed the region.

Bones and skeletons of these ancient animals are still being discovered today. For example, a major fossil deposit was found near Johnson City in 2000. Workers building a road were surprised when their

Tennessee mountaineers lived simply with few comforts.

machinery uncovered the remains of mastodons, horses, tapirs, giant sloths, and turtles. Bones from a giant beaver were also found at the spot. The bones show that the beaver may have been as large as a car.

The first people probably arrived in Tennessee about 15,000 years ago. These people hunted and fished. They also gathered wild berries and nuts for food. They didn't live in villages. When food became scarce, they moved on. The only clues they left behind were rough stone tools, spear points, and arrowheads.

A few thousand years ago, Native Americans came into the area now called Tennessee. They lived along the rivers where they ate shellfish and hunted animals. After a period of time, they started to grow food such as squash and gourds. Because they could now grow their food, they began to stay in one place and live in villages.

The Pinson Mounds area covers about 1,162 acres and includes twelve mounds.

About one thousand years ago, a group of Native Americans called the Mound Builders lived in the region. These people farmed the land, growing corn and beans. As their population increased, they organized themselves into tribes and built towns. They also built huge earthen mounds. They constructed their homes and places of worship on top of some of the mounds. They buried their dead in other mounds. Signs of their civilization still exist in Tennessee. A collection of these mounds is called the Pinson Mounds, which are located in southwest Tennessee. These mounds are very high—one reaches seven stories. By the 1500s, the Mound Builders had disappeared. No one knows what happened to them.

EARLY EXPLORATION

The first European explorers found two major Native American tribes living in Tennessee—the Cherokee and the Chickasaw. The Cherokee were a powerful group who lived in the eastern areas, along the Hiwassee and Little Tennessee Rivers. They used upright poles, tree bark, reeds, grasses, and mud to build their houses.

The Cherokee were farmers. They grew corn, squash, and pumpkins. Women tended the farms, and the men hunted woodland animals, such as deer and elk. These animals were used as food and their skins were made into clothing.

The Chickasaw claimed an area west of the Tennessee River. They didn't live in permanent villages. They moved from place to place with the changing of the seasons, building houses near rivers and streams. Chickasaw warriors attacked other tribes who tried to come into their territory. Young boys learned how to be hunters and fierce warriors. Girls helped their mothers in the fields and with the cooking. The Chickasaw ate deer meat as well as bear meat, and made their clothing from animal skins and capes from bird feathers.

Hernando de Soto explored throughout Tennessee, Alabama, Mississippi, and Louisiana.

Spanish explorers were the first Europeans to reach Tennessee. In 1541, Hernando de Soto and his men planted a Spanish flag on the banks of the Mississippi and left. No other Europeans came to the area until more than a century later.

By 1673, other European countries were taking an interest in what is now called Tennessee. English traders from North Carolina, James Needham and Gabriel Arthur, traveled into Tennessee. Others explorers followed. In 1682, René Robert Cavelier, Sieur de La Salle, set up a temporary post on the Chickasaw Bluffs near present-day Memphis. He claimed the entire Mississippi Valley for France. Charles Charleville was another explorer who came into Tennessee. In 1714, he built a fort at a

In 1682 La Salle claimed the entire Mississippi Valley for France.

place called French Lick. The fort served as a center of the fur-trading business. Later, the city of Nashville developed near Fort Lick.

Late in the seventeenth century, English fur traders came over the Appalachian Mountains into Tennessee. They competed with the French for the fur trade. The Native Americans exchanged animal furs for guns and cooking utensils. Furs from deer and beaver were worth a great deal of money. The traders shipped the furs to Europe to be made into clothing such as hats and coats. Some of the early fur traders were Alexander Cummings, James Adair, and Martin Chartier. They carried animal skins to Charles Town, South Carolina, or shipped them down the Mississippi to New Orleans. At this time, merchants in South Carolina controlled the fur trade in Tennessee. For example, in 1748 about 160,000 skins, worth $250,000, were sent to Europe.

In 1754, the French and Indian War (1754–1763) broke out between England and France. Both countries wanted ownership of North America. Native Americans were also brought into the war, taking sides with either the French or the English.

In 1756 the English built Fort Loudoun near where Vonore is now located. The fort was on the banks of the Little Tennessee River. The French encouraged the Cherokee to attack it. In 1760 Cherokee warriors surrounded the fort. Cut off from getting food supplies, the starving people in

During the French and Indian War, Tennessee settlers crossed the mountains to fight the French.

the fort were forced to eat their horses. Finally, they surrendered and were killed.

When the war ended in 1763, England gained control of all the land claimed by France east of the Mississippi. The region of Tennessee then became part of England's colony of North Carolina. In order to keep people in the colonies from moving westward, England issued the Proclamation of 1763. This law said that no colonists could settle west of the Appalachian Mountains.

FIRST SETTLERS

Many settlers from Virginia and North Carolina disobeyed the proclamation. They moved across the mountains into the lush, green valleys of eastern Tennessee. A North Carolina merchant made a deal with the Cherokees to buy a huge section of their land. He was able to buy about 20 million acres of Cherokee land for about $50,000. Many Cherokees and members of other tribes disagreed with the land sale and prepared to fight any settlers who came into Tennessee.

By the early 1770s there were four small settlements in Tennessee—on the Watauga River, the North Holston, the Nolichucky, and in Carter's Valley. Under the leadership of North Carolinian William Bean, they formed the Watauga Association to govern themselves. This was the first non-Native American settlement in Tennessee. They wrote the Watauga Compact as a form of self-government.

These people were not traders. They wanted to be landowners. One of the largest pioneer groups consisted of about three hundred people who came in 1779. They built the town of Nashborough, which later became the city of Nashville.

By 1780, colonists had been fighting for their independence from England for five years in the Revolutionary War (1775–1783). The southern colonies were almost completely under English command. However, the settlements in the mountains of Tennessee, Virginia, and North Carolina were far away from the war and the English. The English threat to take the "overmountain" territories pushed the pioneers into action.

On September 25, 1780, more than a thousand frontier men gathered at what is now the town of Elizabethton. Here, they made preparations for the 180-mile (290-km) journey across the mountains to find the British. It was quite a scene. Instead of tailored uniforms, these frontier fighters wore wide-brimmed hats, shirts of buckskin (made from deer hide), and breeches (trousers) of home-dyed cloth. Wives and children came to bid the men good-bye. They milled about with the horses and cattle.

Nashville was started in 1779 when James Robertson, an Englishman, set up a settlement on the bank of the Cumberland River. The settlement was called Nashborough in honor of Francis Nash, a general in the Revolutionary War.

FAMOUS FIRSTS

- First example of non-Native American self-government in the United States—Watauga Association
- First anti-slavery paper published in Jonesborough
- First Confederate state to be readmitted to the United States
- First U.S. Navy admiral
- First Coca-Cola bottled in Chattanooga
- First miniature golf course in Chattanooga

FIND OUT MORE

In what ways might life have been different for James Sevier than it is for you?

An incident occurred on that autumn day that would be spoken of again and again. James Sevier, one of John Sevier's ten children by his first wife, longed to go to fight the English soldiers with his brother. However, fifteen-year-old James had no horse. The boy's stepmother said to her husband, "Here, Mr. Sevier, is another of your boys who wants to go with his father and brother Joseph to the war; but we have no horse for him, and, poor fellow, it is too great a distance for him to walk." Sevier found a horse for his young son. James, riding horseback, joined the others on the long march to King's Mountain.

On October 7, 1780, the Tennesseans fought the English in South Carolina. Under the leadership of John Sevier, they helped win the Battle of King's Mountain. In the end, the colonies won the war. In 1783, they formed a new country—the United States of America.

Tennessee troops defeated the British at King's Mountain.

THE SIXTEENTH STATE

After the Revolutionary War, Tennessee remained a part of the state of North Carolina. However, some of the people in eastern Tennessee were not happy. They thought that North Carolina was too far away and didn't pay attention to the needs and dangers of the backcountry. In 1784, a group of people set up their own state called Franklin, which was named for Benjamin Franklin. John Sevier served as governor. Franklin was short-lived. There were bitter arguments between those who remained loyal to North Carolina and the Franklinites. The Cherokees increased their raids on the weakened settlement. By 1788, the state of Franklin didn't exist. The people were again under North Carolina rule. In 1790, the U.S. Congress made Tennessee a United States territory.

A special census in 1795 showed that 77,262 people lived in the territory. The population was more than enough to apply for statehood. On June 1, 1796, Congress admitted Tennessee as the sixteenth state of the United States. Knoxville was made the capital. Tennessee chose Sevier again as governor. They also adopted a state constitution and elected Andrew Jackson, a lawyer, to the U.S. Congress.

As soon as Tennessee became a state, more and more settlers came. They came from other states along the eastern seaboard and from countries in Europe. The United States entered yet another war with England, the War of 1812

FIND OUT MORE

A constitution is a written document that describes how the government of a nation or state will be set up and the duties of those responsible for running the government. Why is a constitution important?

(1812–1815). Just as in the French and Indian War and the Revolutionary War, the War of 1812 involved the Native Americans. American frontiersmen moved onto land claimed by the British, while the British and their Indian allies fought back. General Andrew Jackson defeated the Creeks in 1814 at Horseshoe Bend in present-day Alabama. This was the first of two battles that made Jackson a national hero. In 1815, Jackson and the Tennessee volunteers defeated a large group of English soldiers in the Battle of New Orleans. Because of his toughness in battle, Andrew Jackson was nicknamed "Old Hickory."

Andrew Jackson was elected President in 1828. Unlike the first six presidents who came from wealthy families, Jackson was a frontiersman. As President, Jackson backed efforts to move Native Americans from their land to make room for settlers. During Jackson's presidency, the U.S. Government passed the Indian Removal Act of 1830. Under this law, Native Americans living in the East were to be moved to an area called "Indian Territory" in what is now the state of Oklahoma. The most affected group in Tennessee was the Cherokee.

The year before the Indian Removal Act of 1830, gold was discovered on Cherokee lands in present-day northeast Georgia. White miners illegally invaded the area, hoping to get rich quick. The Cherokees appealed to the courts for justice. Finally, the case was taken before the U.S. Supreme Court. Chief Justice John Marshall ruled in favor of the Cherokees. However, President Jackson declared, "John Marshall has made his decision; let him enforce it, if he can."

Though the Cherokees had a permanent settlement, built their own schools, printed their own books, and even published a newspaper, they were forced to leave their land. Nearly a thousand Cherokees hid in the Smoky Mountains, where their descendants live today. The rest of the Cherokees, as many as 14,000, started the long trip in the fall of 1838. The old and disabled rode in wagons, along with small children. A few Cherokee rode horses. The rest walked. Most left their homes

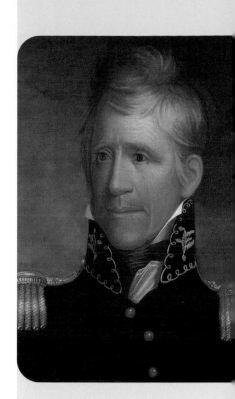

Andrew Jackson fought Native Americans nearly all his life. As president, he was finally able to get the U.S. Congress to pass a law that removed the Cherokee from their land.

Many Cherokee died on the "Trail of Tears."

with only the clothing on their backs. They suffered in the freezing rain and blinding snowstorms. At each night's stop, the Cherokees buried those who had died that day. At least one out of every four Cherokees died of hunger, cold, or disease along the way. It was a cruel journey with much weeping and moaning. That is why the route was called the "Trail of Tears."

THE CIVIL WAR

By 1860 the North and the South had developed into two very different regions. In the North, businesses, mills, and factories were built where people were paid wages for their work. In the South, most people worked in farming. Cotton was the major crop grown there. African-American slaves did much of the hard work on farms and plantations. Slaves were not considered citizens. They were treated as property, and could be bought or sold like a horse or a wagon. In the North, slavery was illegal.

Here is how one slave described her life in the South: "We lodged in log huts and on the bare ground. In a single room were huddled, like cattle, ten or a dozen persons, men, women, and children. Our beds were collections of straw and old rags, thrown down in the corners and boxed in with boards, a single blanket the only covering."

Tennessee—like the nation—was divided over the issue of slavery. In 1860, Tennessee's population was over one million people. Of this number, 275,000 were slaves. Large farms with thousands of acres called plantations in West and Middle Tennessee needed many laborers to produce cotton and tobacco. Slaves provided the labor. In East Tennessee, the farms were small and had few, if any, slaves. Most people in East Tennessee thought slavery was wrong.

Abraham Lincoln was elected President in 1860. He promised to keep the nation united and to keep slavery out of the new western territories. The South felt threatened by this. They believed each state should make its own laws and didn't want the U.S. government to interfere with their way of life. As a result, seven southern states seceded, or broke away, from the nation before Lincoln took office. They formed a new country—the Confederate States of America.

Tennesseans did not consider secession until Confederate soldiers attacked Fort Sumter, a U.S. fort in South Carolina. Though a majority of Tennesseans voted to secede, most of East Tennessee voted against secession. Tennessee became the last of the eleven southern states to join the Confederacy on June 8, 1861. Tennessee sent men to fight on both sides of the Civil War—about 115,000 Confederate soldiers and 30,000 Union soldiers. Union and Confederate armies crossed the state many times, fighting battle after battle on Tennessee soil.

EXTRA! EXTRA!

Sam Davis, at the age of 21, was tried and hanged as a Confederate spy during the Civil War. He came to be known as the "boy hero of the Confederacy." Union soldiers offered to spare his life if he would name the person who gave him information. Davis replied, "I would die a thousand deaths before I would betray a friend."

Families from one end of the state to the other suffered hardships. Sixteen-year-old Alice Williamson of Gallatin kept a diary. On June 10, 1864, she wrote about the Union soldiers who took over her home: "The country is overrun with Yanks. They are camped in the woods in front of us and have already paid us several visits and killed sheep, goats and chickens. Some came today and demanded their dinner at two o'clock but did not get it."

More battles were fought in Tennessee than in any other state except Virginia. At least six major battles and hundreds of skirmishes were fought in the Volunteer State. The battles of Fort Donelson, Shiloh, Stones River, Chattanooga, Franklin, and Nashville destroyed much property and took many lives.

The battle of Shiloh was one of the bloodiest battles of the Civil War.

The Battle of Shiloh began on April 6, 1862. Confederate General Albert Sidney Johnston led an attack against Union General Ulysses S. Grant's forces at Shiloh Church. When their general was hit, the Confederates stopped their attack. The next morning the Union forces attacked the Confederates. The Confederates retreated toward Corinth, Mississippi. About 23,746 Union and Confederate soldiers died during the battle.

The battle of Chickamauga Creek resulted in heavy losses for both Union and Confederate forces.

On September 19, 1863, a battle was fought at Chickamauga Creek. At stake was the city of Chattanooga, which was an important railroad center. Confederate soldiers won the battle and drove Union forces to the city of Chattanooga. Then the Confederates surrounded the city. On November 25 another battle took place at Chattanooga when General Grant and his Union troops marched into the area. During the battle, the Union soldiers forced the Confederates to withdraw. More than 48,000 soldiers were killed in these battles.

The Civil War ended on April 9, 1865 with the surrender of the Confederate Army. Five days later, President Abraham

EXTRA! EXTRA!

The first admiral in U.S. history was a Tennessean. David Farragut (1801–1870) joined the navy at age nine. During the War of 1812, twelve-year-old Farragut captured an enemy ship. After his victory at Mobile Bay during the Civil War, he became an admiral, the first in the U.S. Navy.

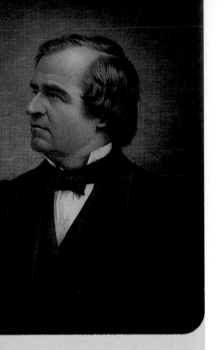

Andrew Johnson never attended school. He was a tailor before he was elected to the U.S. Congress and then governor of Tennessee.

Lincoln was shot. After Lincoln's death, the vice-president, Andrew Johnson of Tennessee, became the seventeenth president of the United States.

RECONSTRUCTION

After the war, Tennessee, along with the other Confederate states, was in ruins. Tennesseans began the task of building new towns, homes, factories, roads, and railways. Many people left their burned plantations and ruined farms and moved to the cities.

The 250,000 African-American Tennesseans who had been slaves in 1860 were no longer property. Lincoln had issued the Emancipation Proclamation of 1863. It freed all slaves in the Confederacy, but it did not apply to states under Union control. Tennessee was one of those states. In February 1865, Tennessee became the only one of the seceded states to free slaves by its own act—an amendment to the state constitution. In July 1866, Tennessee approved the Fourteenth Amendment to the Constitution of the United States. This amendment guaranteed basic political rights to all U.S. citizens. Tennessee, the last state to leave the Union, became the first state to rejoin on July 24, 1866.

After the Civil War, African-Americans were in a more unsettled condition than were most other Tennesseans. They had no

EXTRA! EXTRA!

Three United States presidents were from Tennessee:
- Andrew Jackson (1767–1845) was the seventh president
- James Knox Polk (1795–1849) was the eleventh president
- Andrew Johnson (1808–1875) was the seventeenth president

land of their own. Many took jobs working for people who had once been their owners. African-Americans sometimes rented a piece of large plantations and farmed it. This was called tenant farming. Others worked as sharecroppers. They worked the owner's land for an agreed share of the crop. Sharecroppers had to pay the landowner for the seed they planted and for any tools they used. When the crop was sold, these costs were taken away from the profits so that most sharecroppers received little or no money. Because they had few opportunities in farming, large numbers of African-Americans left rural areas, pouring into cities like Memphis, Chattanooga, Nashville, and Knoxville.

African-Americans also faced threats of violence. Many white Southerners didn't want African-Americans to exercise their new rights under the U.S Constitution. These white people formed secret groups to threaten African-Americans. One of these groups was the Ku Klux Klan. The Klan was organized in Pulaski in 1865.

Thousands of Southern white people joined the Klan. Klan members used violence to keep African-Americans from voting or holding public office. Klan members often struck during the night. They burned homes and businesses. They attacked, beat,

Ku Klux Klan members usually wore masks and white robes.

and killed African-Americans. Klan members also lynched—or put to death by hanging—African-Americans.

By the 1880s, whites who wanted to limit the rights of African-Americans gained control of the Tennessee government. Tennessee passed laws, called Jim Crow laws, that kept African-Americans from using the same public facilities as white people. African-Americans had to attend separate schools and ride in separate railroad cars. They had to use separate restaurants, restrooms, drinking fountains, hotels, and cemeteries. In 1890 the Tennessee legislature passed a poll tax law. Only African-Americans who paid the tax would be allowed to vote. However, many of them could not afford the tax and so could not vote. In order to escape these laws and the threats of death, many African-Americans left Tennessee and migrated to the North.

By the late 1880s, growing numbers of Tennesseans had left their farms and moved to towns and cities. At this time, farmers were not getting good prices for their crops and they were going into debt to buy new farm equipment. Many farmers left their farms to seek jobs elsewhere. After the Civil War, new businesses and industries from the North moved into Tennessee. Many people worked in cotton and woolen mills. A major ironworks was built at Rockwood. A huge iron and steel industry blossomed in Chattanooga, which helped the city become a major industrial center in the South. Others worked in lumber and flour milling industries. More coal mines opened in the mountains of East Tennessee.

As the nineteenth century drew to an end, sixteen out of every hundred Tennesseans lived in cities. The largest city was Memphis, with about 102,000 people. In 1897 Tennesseans threw a big party in Nashville. It was Tennessee's 100th birthday —a year late. The Centennial Exposition displayed the state's progress. About two million people came to the exposition during the six months that it was open. The most beautiful attraction was a building called the Parthenon, an exact copy of the Greek temple by the same name.

Many people found work in the Iron Works at Rockwood in the 1880s.

BEGINNING OF THE TWENTIETH CENTURY

In 1917, the United States entered World War I (1914–1918). As usual, the people of Tennessee contributed to the war effort. Farmers and factory workers produced goods to aid U.S. soldiers fighting against Germany in Europe. New factories opened, such as a gunpowder plant near Nashville. Almost 100,000 Tennesseans served in the armed forces. About 61,000 Tennesseans were drafted into the Army—17,000 of them were African-Americans. They served in units separate from whites and were commanded by white officers. Nurses volunteered for duty in the Red Cross and many served in France and England.

Tennessee provided the most celebrated U.S. soldier of World War I—Alvin C. York. In 1917 York joined the All-American Division. All alone, he captured 132 German soldiers and killed twenty-five in the Argonne Forest on October 8, 1918. He received medals for bravery from both the United States and France.

A major issue during the early 1900s focused on the voting rights of women. In 1906 the Tennessee Equal Suffrage Association formed. The word *suffrage* means "the right to vote." Many people in Tennessee were against women's suffrage, including many women. However, women gained some voting rights in Tennessee before they did in other parts of the country. In 1920 all the state legislatures considered the Nineteenth Amendment to the U.S. Constitution, which would allow women to vote. If two-thirds of the states agreed to the amendment, then it would become law. Tennessee agreed to the Nineteenth Amendment when Harry Burn, a legislator, switched sides. He had received a telegram from his mother that encouraged him to vote for the Amendment and he did. With Tennessee's approval, the amendment became law.

Tennessee's Alvin York was the most decorated soldier of World War I.

Tennessee received more attention in 1925 with the Scopes trial, which became known as the "Monkey Trial." John Scopes, a biology teacher in Dayton, was arrested for teaching the theory of evolution to high school students. The theory of evolution says that humans developed over a long period of time from simpler forms of life. A few weeks before his arrest, the Tennessee legislature made the teaching of evolution illegal. The trial became like a circus as people came from all over the country to see it. Newspapers carried many articles about the trial. Scopes was finally found guilty and fined $100. Teaching about evolution in Tennessee's schools was illegal for the next forty years.

During the 1920s new kinds of music became popular in Tennessee and swept across the country. In 1925, WSM, a powerful radio station in Nashville, started broadcasting the "Grand Ole Opry." All kinds of musicians performed on the program each week—banjo players from the mountains, church gospel singers, and funny comic acts. Country music quickly became popular.

In 1927 Victor Records went into the rural areas of Tennessee to make records with Jimmie Rodgers and the Carter family. For the first time, people could buy records that featured popular country singers and musicians. Tennessee became the center of country music, where many entertainers lived.

Tennessee became the center for another kind of music, too—the blues. Memphis, in particular, became a hot spot for the blues. Performers came in from the farms to play their music in the clubs on Beale

John Scopes was found guilty of teaching the theory of evolution. Here, he receives the judge's sentence.

Street. W.C. Handy, a Beale Street musician, wrote and published the "Memphis Blues." This was the first blues music ever published. Another blues pioneer of the 1920s was Bessie Smith, who sang at many Beale Street clubs.

THE GREAT DEPRESSION

Four years after the Scopes trial, the Great Depression hit the country. The Great Depression started when the stock market crashed in October, 1929. A depression is a time when many businesses fail and many people do not have jobs. During the Great Depression (1929–1939), factories, banks, and mines closed all over the United States. One out of every four people was out of work.

The Great Depression was devastating for the United States—and Tennessee. During World War I, farmers had been getting high prices for their cotton crops. After the war, there were fewer markets and prices fell. Then, a drought, a period of little or no rain, destroyed many of the crops. In addition, the use of tractors and mechanical cotton pickers meant that farmers needed fewer helpers. Many farmers went to the cities to find work. Some worked for the DuPont factory in Old Hickory or the Eastman-Kodak factory in Kingsport. Others found work at the Aluminum Company of America factory in Blount County. When the Great Depression hit, these factories cut production as well as the number of workers.

The Great Depression was a time of suffering. Some people wandered from city to city looking for work. They lined up at churches and at other places that provided free food. In the country, people collected walnuts to sell. Others lived on scraps found in garbage cans.

When Franklin D. Roosevelt became President, he promised a New Deal for the American people. In 1933 the U.S. government started programs to help put people back to work. One program in Tennessee was the Tennessee Valley Authority (TVA). Through the TVA program, workers built dams and locks on the Tennessee River. The dams controlled flooding. Power plants built by the TVA brought cheap electricity to about 60,000 farm families across the state. Before this, most

Norris Dam on the Clinch River was the first dam built under the TVA.

homes had no electricity. Lakes created behind the dams were then used for fishing and boating. Thanks to the TVA projects, Tennessee fared better during the Great Depression than some of its neighboring states.

WORLD WAR II

The Great Depression eased with the coming of World War II (1939–1945). The second huge war of the twentieth century began in 1939 with Germany's attack on other European countries. The United States entered World War II in 1941 after Japan attacked Pearl Harbor, a U.S. naval base in Hawaii.

Tennessee played a major role in World War II. More than 309,000 Tennesseans fought in the war. Factories in the state made weapons and aircraft. While men fought in Europe and in the Pacific Ocean, more and more women took jobs in factories back in the U.S.

Several Tennesseans played important roles in the U.S. government at this time. Joseph W. Byrns, who was from Robertson County, became Speaker of the U.S. House of Representatives. Kenneth D. McKellar of Memphis served six straight terms in the U.S. Senate from 1916–1952. Cordell Hull was from Celina. He was a member of the U.S. Congress from 1907 to 1933. Hull then served as Secretary of State for President Franklin D. Roosevelt.

In the early 1940s the U.S. government created the town of Oak Ridge. About 70,000 people came to live there. At Oak Ridge scientists worked in secret to help build the first atomic bombs. These bombs were more powerful than any that had ever been invented. In 1945 the United States dropped two atomic bombs on Japan, which brought about the end of the war.

After 1945, returning servicemen and women helped bring about more change in Tennessee. Ex-servicemen had no desire to return to back-breaking farm labor. They wanted to move to the cities and find jobs in factories and businesses. Many women who had worked in factories during the war years continued to work.

During World War II, many women worked in factories. These women are sewing Army shirts.

CHANGE COMES TO TENNESSEE

In the 1950s and 1960s, African-Americans were determined not to accept the attacks and lynchings that had occurred in their communities in the past. They used peaceful methods to bring about change. Organized groups of African-Americans tried to be served at lunch counters that only served white people. Protestors sat down, blocked entrances, and refused to move until they were served. These protests came to be known as sit-ins. In Nashville and elsewhere, police often dragged the protestors out and put them in jail.

A woman stands in front of the entrance to a Memphis lunch counter to prevent African-Americans from taking seats.

In 1954, the Supreme Court ruled that "whites only" schools were against the law of the land—the U.S. Constitution. Some Southern states were slow to follow the Court ruling. However, Tennessee began allowing African-Americans to attend white schools in 1956. The state government sent troops to schools to protect African-American children from harrassment.

New state laws were passed that made segregation, or separation, of African-Americans illegal. However, although African-Americans could use libraries, restaurants, rest rooms, and other public places by the mid-1960s, racial unrest remained. On April 4, 1968, a tragic event took place in Tennessee. Civil rights leader Dr. Martin Luther King Jr. traveled to Memphis to help garbage workers get higher pay and better working conditions. Outside his hotel, Dr. King was shot and killed.

The 1950s and 1960s brought other kinds of changes, too. New businesses and factories came to the state. Thousands of farm families moved off the farms to take jobs in factories. In 1960 the number of people living in cities was greater than the number of those living in small towns. During the 1980s, people and new industries from the north surged to the state. In 1982, the World's Fair was held in Knoxville. The fair brought thousands of tourists from all over the world to Tennessee. The fair also brought millions of dollars to the state.

The Tombigbee Waterway, connecting the Tennessee River and the Gulf of Mexico, was opened in the 1980s. Now that Tennessee had better shipping lanes, more industry and trade came to the state. General Motors began manufacturing Saturn automobiles in Spring Hill. Foreign industries also began locating in the state. Nissan, a Japanese company, opened an automobile manufacturing plant in Smyrna.

By 1994, there were sixty-nine Japanese manufacturers in Tennessee, which employed tens of thousands of people. Other Japanese-owned companies in Tennessee today include Toshiba American Consumer

Tennessee's Al Gore, the Democratic candidate in the 2000 election, speaks at a rally.

Products in Lebanon, Nakano Foods, Inc. in Crossville, and Sony ATV Tree Music Publishing in Nashville.

In 1993 national attention focused on Tennessee once again when Albert Gore, Jr. became vice president under President Bill Clinton. Gore, who lived in Carthage, had represented Tennessee in both the U.S. Congress and Senate. He was the Democratic presidential candidate in 2000, but lost the election.

Today, Tennessee is a prosperous state. Jobs are plentiful. The average income of Tennesseans is more than double that of a decade earlier. The educational system in Tennessee is considered one of the best in the country. The future, too, looks bright. More industries are planning to build in the state.

CHAPTER FOUR

GOVERNING TENNESSEE

Tennessee has had three state constitutions. Today's government operates under the 1870 constitution. The constitution divides the state government into three parts—executive, legislative, and judicial. The structure of Tennessee's government is similar to that of the government of the United States.

The capitol building is constructed of Tennessee marble.

THE EXECUTIVE BRANCH

The executive branch carries out state laws. The chief executive officer is the governor, who is elected by the people. Other members of the executive branch include the lieutenant governor, the secretary of state, the attorney general, the state treasurer, and the comptroller of treasury. The governor serves a four-year term. He or she may be re-elected for a second term.

The governor's chief duty is to represent the state to the nation and the world. Other duties include preparing the budget, recruiting new industry, promoting tourism, and urging lawmakers to pass laws that are in the best interests of the state. The governor has the power to veto (say no to) a proposed law or bill, but the legislature may override the veto by a majority vote in both houses. The governor also has the power to call out the National Guard in an emergency. The governor appoints department heads to help run the executive branch. They oversee such areas as the environment, education, and economy.

The General Assembly meets regularly to discuss new laws (bills) or changes to existing laws (amendments).

THE LEGISLATIVE BRANCH

Tennessee's legislature makes the laws for the state. The legislative branch is called the General Assembly. The General Assembly is made up of two groups: the Senate and the House of Representatives.

Tennessee's thirty-three senators serve four-year terms. Senators must be at least 30 years old, a U.S. citizen, and a resident of the state for at least three years. The leader of the senate, or speaker, is the lieutenant governor.

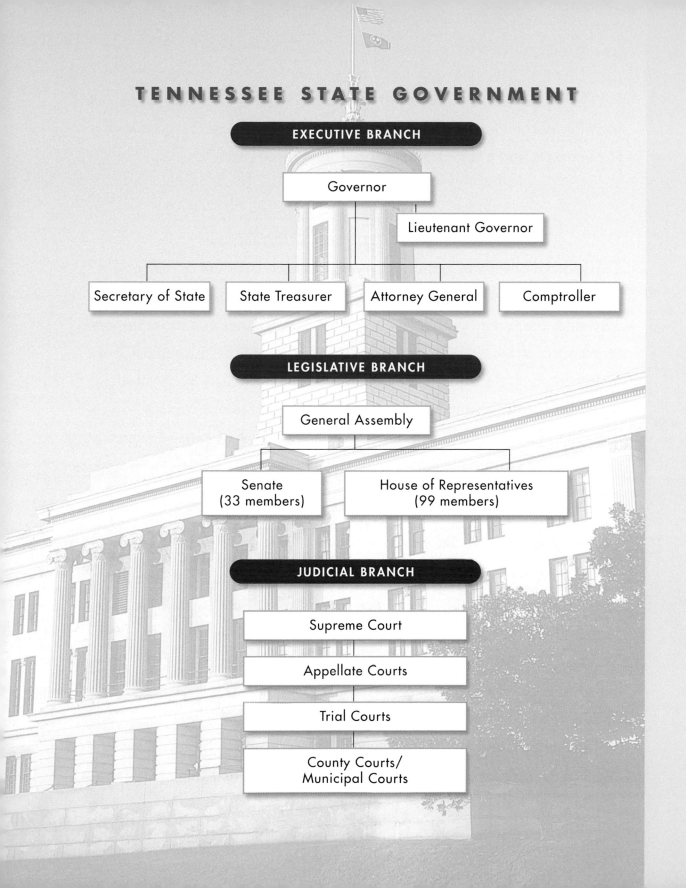

TENNESSEE STATE GOVERNMENT

EXECUTIVE BRANCH

Governor

Lieutenant Governor

Secretary of State

State Treasurer

Attorney General

Comptroller

LEGISLATIVE BRANCH

General Assembly

Senate
(33 members)

House of Representatives
(99 members)

JUDICIAL BRANCH

Supreme Court

Appellate Courts

Trial Courts

County Courts/
Municipal Courts

The ninety-nine representatives are elected for two-year terms. A member of the House of Representatives must be at least 21 years old, a U.S. citizen, and a state resident for at least three years.

THE JUDICIAL BRANCH

The judicial branch of Tennessee's government is a system of courts. The courts explain and interpret the laws passed by the General Assembly. The state Supreme Court, with five judges, is Tennessee's most important court. If a case is disputed in a lower court, the Supreme Court makes the final decision. The five justices are nominated by the Judicial Selection Commission. The governor appoints the people in this organization. Courts below the Supreme Court include the Court of Appeals, the Court of Criminal Appeals, and trial courts.

TAKE A TOUR OF NASHVILLE, THE STATE CAPITAL

Nashville—located on the Cumberland River—became the capital in 1843. Its beginnings date back to the founding of Fort Nashborough by settlers in 1779. Later, the name was changed to Nashville.

The capitol building was designed by William Strickland. He died before the building, modeled after a Greek temple, was completed. His body was buried in a vault in the north wall of the building.

Tennessee stone and marble were used as the main building materials. Construction started in 1845 and was finished 14 years later.

TENNESSEE GOVERNORS

Name	Term	Name	Term
John Sevier	1796–1801	John P. Buchanan	1891–1893
Archibald Roane	1801–1803	Peter Turney	1893–1897
John Sevier	1803–1809	Robert L. Taylor	1897–1899
Willie Blount	1809–1815	Benton McMillin	1899–1903
Joseph McMinn	1815–1821	James B. Frazier	1903–1905
William Carroll	1821–1827	John I. Cox	1905–1907
Sam Houston	1827–1829	Malcolm R. Patterson	1907–1911
William Hall (acting)	1829	Ben W. Hooper	1911–1915
William Carroll	1829–1935	Thomas C. Rye	1915–1919
Newton Cannon	1835–1839	Albert H. Roberts	1919–1921
James K. Polk	1839–1841	Alfred A. Taylor	1921–1923
James C. Jones	1841–1845	Austin Peay	1923–1927
Aaron V. Brown	1845–1847	Henry H. Horton	1927–1933
Neill S. Brown	1847–1849	Hill McAlister	1933–1937
William Trousdale	1849–1851	Gordon Browning	1937–1939
William B. Campbell	1851–1853	Prentice Cooper	1939–1945
Andrew Johnson	1853–1857	Jim Nance McCord	1945–1949
Isham G. Harris	1857–1862	Gordon Browning	1949–1953
Andrew Johnson	1862–1865	Frank G. Clement	1953–1959
William G. Brownlow	1865–1869	Buford Ellington	1959–1963
DeWitt C. Senter	1869–1871	Frank G. Clement	1963–1967
John C. Brown	1871–1875	Buford Ellington	1967–1971
James D. Porter	1875–1879	Winfield Dunn	1971–1975
Albert S. Marks	1879–1881	Ray Blanton	1975–1979
Alvin Hawkins	1881–1883	Lamar Alexander	1979–1987
William B. Bate	1883–1887	Ned R. McWherter	1987–1995
Robert L. Taylor	1887–1891	Don Sundquist	1995–

This scene shows the Nashville skyline.

Repairs in recent years have returned Tennessee's State Capitol to its original beauty. The governor's offices and the chambers of the Senate and the House of Representatives are in the capitol building.

The magnificent capitol stands on a steep hill, overlooking the city. It features massive columns. On top of the building's tower is an enormous lantern. The building is almost as long as a football field. The height of the building from the ground to the top of the tower nearly equals its length. The tomb of James K. Polk, eleventh president of the United States, is on the state capitol grounds. Statues on the grounds include President Andrew Jackson, Sam Davis, and Alvin C. York.

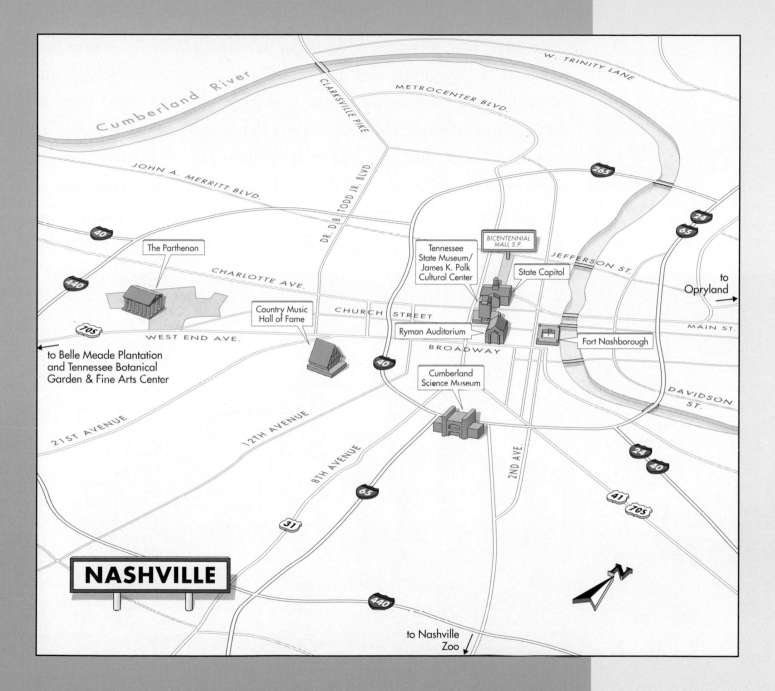

The Parthenon

Tennessee State Museum/James K. Polk Cultural Center

BICENTENNIAL MALL S.P.

State Capitol

Country Music Hall of Fame

Ryman Auditorium

Fort Nashborough

to Belle Meade Plantation and Tennessee Botanical Garden & Fine Arts Center

Cumberland Science Museum

to Opryland

Cumberland River

CLARKSVILLE PIKE

W. TRINITY LANE

METROCENTER BLVD.

JOHN A. MERRITT BLVD.

DR. D.B. TODD JR. BLVD.

JEFFERSON ST.

CHARLOTTE AVE.

CHURCH STREET

MAIN ST.

WEST END AVE.

BROADWAY

DAVIDSON ST.

21ST AVENUE

12TH AVENUE

8TH AVENUE

2ND AVE.

NASHVILLE

to Nashville Zoo

40 440 705 65 31 440 24 40 41 705 65 24 265

N

In 1897 Tennessee celebrated its one hundredth birthday. A large fair was held at Centennial Park in Nashville. A new building called the Parthenon was the main attraction. It is the world's only exact copy of the ancient Parthenon temple in Greece that was used by worshipers of Athena, a Greek goddess. Inside the building is a 42-foot (12.8-m) statue of Athena. This statue is the tallest indoor sculpture in the United States. After the centennial celebration, people called Nashville the "Athens of the South." Nashville's Parthenon is now used as a museum.

The Parthenon was originally built in 1897 and rebuilt in 1929. The building does not have a single straight line, and no two columns are the same size.

The Tennessee Bicentennial Capitol Mall was built to honor Tennessee's 200th birthday in 1996. The Mall covers nineteen acres. It provides learning experiences for all ages. A 200-foot granite map of the state, believed to be the largest state map ever made, sparkles with tiny lights at night. The lights indicate the ninety-five county seats.

There is much more to see and do in Nashville. You can visit Fort Nashborough. The fort has been rebuilt to show what life was like at the time of the founding of Nashville. The Tennessee State Museum tells the history of Tennessee through many exhibits. Highlights include a log cabin and the hat that Andrew Jackson wore to his presidential ceremonies. The Tennessee Botanical Gardens and Fine Arts Center is for nature lovers. Fans of country music will enjoy a visit to Ryman Auditorium.

Nashville visitors like to visit Ryman Auditorium, where the original Grand Ole Opry concerts took place.

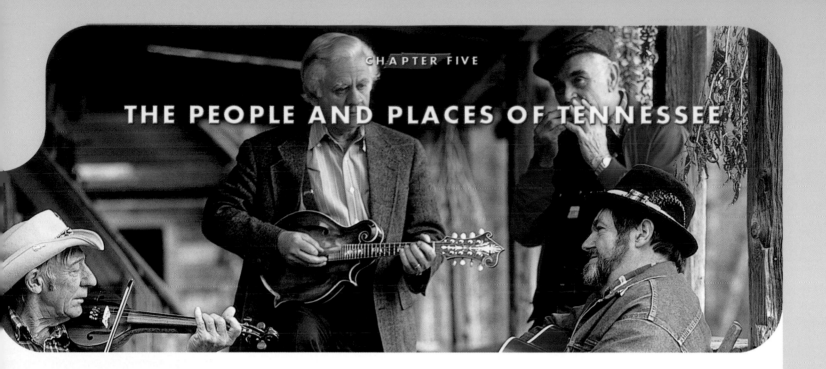

CHAPTER FIVE

THE PEOPLE AND PLACES OF TENNESSEE

Anywhere that people get together in Tennessee, country music will likely be heard.

From the mountains to the shores of the Mississippi, the people of Tennessee agree on one thing: they love music! In East Tennessee, the favorites are ballads and bluegrass music. Country music was born in Middle Tennessee. Rock and roll and blues music began in West Tennessee. Music fills the air in both small towns and large cities.

MEET THE PEOPLE

Almost six million people live in Tennessee. In recent years, the rural population has dropped. Today, more than six out of ten Tennesseans live in or near cities. Memphis, Nashville, Knoxville, and Chattanooga are the largest cities.

Most people living in Tennessee do not come from other countries. They were born in the state or other parts of the United States. Today,

Tennessee is made up of a mixture of people. More than half the population is concentrated around major metropolitan areas.

about eight out of ten Tennesseans trace their roots to Europeans—English, Scotch-Irish, French, or Germans. Many people who retire from their jobs in other states come to live in Tennessee.

WORKING IN TENNESSEE

Until recent years, most Tennesseans worked on farms. Today, Tennessee is a leading manufacturing state due mainly to the development of cheap electricity and improved transportation.

Many Tennesseans find work in automobile factories.

By the end of the twentieth century about three out of ten people worked in service industries such as hotels, motels, health care or restaurants. Other service industries include education, trade, and banking. Thousands of Tennesseans work at U.S. Government and state government offices. Thousands of others work in the music business.

Almost half a million Tennesseans work in manufacturing. Most manufacturing is found in the eastern part of the state. Chemicals—ranging from medicines to soaps—are Tennessee's major products. Most of the chemical factories are found in Knoxville and Chattanooga. Processed foods such as meat, soft drinks, and breads are in second place. Other leading products

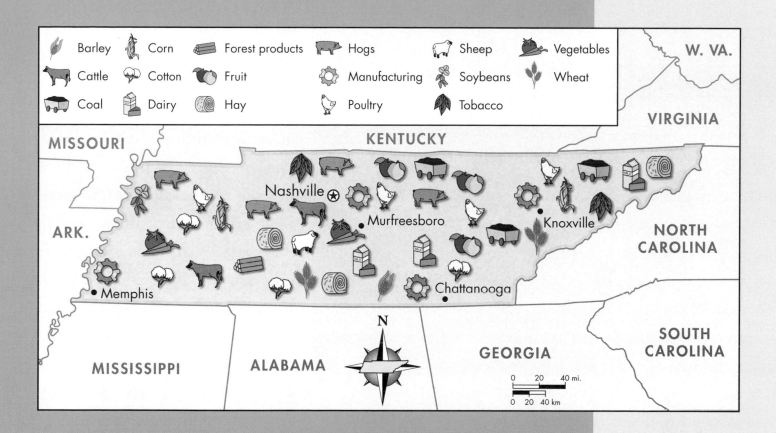

Large harvesting machines are used to bring in the soybean crop.

include clothing, machinery, electronic equipment, and metals. Printing and publishing, as well as clay and glass products, are also important.

The largest cities are the leading manufacturing centers, but manufacturing is found in many smaller cities as well. Alcoa is the site of a large aluminum plant. Book printing plants are located in Kingsport. Factories in Union City turn out tires. Automobiles roll off assembly lines in Smyrna and Spring Hill.

Although farming has declined, many Tennesseans still work on farms. Today, the state has about 80,000 farms. A little less than half of the state's land area is in farms. More tobacco and soybeans are produced now than cotton. Other crops include wheat, corn, apples, strawberries, and tomatoes. Farm income also comes from dairying and raising of livestock.

Coal is mined in the mountains of East Tennessee. The state also produces copper, crushed stone, and marble. Tennessee leads the nation in the mining of zinc.

This is an aerial view of Memphis, the largest port city on the Mississippi River.

TAKE A TOUR OF TENNESSEE

From the Mississippi River in the west to the mountains in the east, there is something for everyone to see and do in the Volunteer State. Six major interstate highways make it easy to get around in Tennessee.

West Tennessee

What better place to start a tour of Tennessee than Memphis! Tennessee's largest city, located in the southwestern corner of the state, overlooks the Mississippi River.

From its earliest times, Memphis has been an important port city involved in cotton trading and shipping. Today, many of the residents work in factories that produce furniture and steel.

WHO'S WHO IN TENNESSEE?

Frederick Wallace Smith (1944–) founded the Memphis-based delivery company, Federal Express Corporation. Federal Express delivers packages around the world.

MISSOURI

ILLINOIS

KENTUCKY

N

W. VA.

VIRGINIA

0   20   40 mi.

0   20   40 km

ARK.

LAND
BETWEEN
THE LAKES

BIG SOUTH FORK NAT'L RIVER
AND RECREATION AREA

CHEROKEE
NAT'L FOREST

Union City

24   65

40

Cookeville

Oak
Ridge

75   Cumberland Gap
Nat'l Historical
Park

81

Nashville

Murfreesboro

Knoxville

40

NORTH
CAROLINA

40

65

GREAT SMOKY MTS.
NAT'L PARK

Jackson

24

75

Lewisburg

Shelbyville

CHEROKEE
NAT'L FOREST

Memphis

Chickamauga and
Chattanooga
Nat'l Military Park

Chattanooga

MISSISSIPPI

ALABAMA

GEORGIA

National park, forest
or recreation area

Highway

Capital city

City

Tourist site

The Pyramid is 32-story stainless steel structure.

The most striking landmark in Memphis is the gleaming steel Pyramid Arena built in 1991 on the banks of the Mississippi River. The base is as wide as six football fields. About 20,000 people can find seats in the arena. It is home to the University of Memphis men's basketball team.

Memphis's Beale Street is the home of the blues. The city is also known as the birthplace of rock and roll music. Singer Elvis Presley made his first records here. Each year about 700,000 people visit Graceland, Elvis Presley's mansion. Graceland has more visitors than any other house in the United States—except the White House in Washington, D.C.

Beale Street is the home of blues music.

Visitors to Graceland are no longer allowed to take photos. Over the years, the flashing cameras have caused fabrics in the rooms to fade.

Memphis is also home to the Brooks Museum of Art. The 7,000 works of art include American portraits and sculptures. The National Civil Rights Museum is located in the Lorraine Hotel in Memphis. Here, visitors can see the balcony where Dr. Martin Luther King was assassinated. The museum contains displays of key events in the civil rights movement of the 1950s and 1960s.

No visitor to Memphis should miss a parade of the famous mallard ducks at the Peabody Hotel. At eleven o'clock every morning, the ducks take the elevator from their rooftop shelter to the lobby. To the strains of band music, the ducks waddle across the red carpet to the fountain. Here, they frolic until five o'clock—then back to the rooftop. This parade of the Peabody ducks has been going on since the 1930s.

Twice a day the ducks parade through the Peabody Hotel.

Shiloh is often the scene of Civil War re-enactments. People dress as Civil War soldiers and act out the battle.

North of Memphis is Reelfoot Lake, a popular spot for fishing and bird watching. East of Memphis is the site of Shiloh National Military Park. This battlefield saw some of the bloodiest fighting of the Civil War.

Middle Tennessee

Millions of visitors come to Nashville each year to enjoy the sights and sounds of Music City, USA. Many famous musicians have made recordings in Nashville such as Dolly Parton and Garth Brooks. Nashville's Grand Ole Opry radio and stage show is the longest running live radio show in the world. The popular radio show celebrated its seventy-fifth birthday in October 2000 with performances by such country music stars as Garth Brooks, Loretta Lynn, Dolly Parton, and Travis Tritt.

Bill Monroe, the father of bluegrass music, entertains on the stage of the Grand Ole Opry.

Homemade, mouthwatering apple crisp is one of the best ways to sample one of Tennessee's leading fruits. Remember to ask an adult for help!

TENNESSEE APPLE CRISP

1 cup water
1-1/2 to 2 tsp. cinnamon
4 cups peeled, sliced apples
1 cup of flour
1 cup of sugar
1 stick butter or margarine
9 x 13 inch baking dish

1. Mix water with cinnamon a little at a time.
2. Place the sliced apples in a baking dish.
3. Pour the cinnamon and water mixture over apples.
4. Mix the flour, sugar, and butter with your hands until the mixture is crumbly.
5. Sprinkle it over the top of the apples.
6. Bake for 40 to 45 minutes at 350°.

Music is only one of Nashville's many attractions. The Tennessee State Museum in downtown Nashville has more than 60,000 square feet (5574 sq m) of exhibits. The exhibits begin by showing life as it may have been 15,000 years ago and continuing to the present. The museum also has large collections of silver, quilts, and furniture from pioneer days.

You may want to stop in the Nashville Toy Museum. It includes hundreds of toy trains, boats, metal soldiers, dolls, and bears. The Wildlife Park at Grassmere includes a zoo, a working farm, and a playground. The working farm teaches about the importance of farm animals to the development of Tennessee. At any one time, about 1,000 children can play in the park's playground, called the Jungle Gym. It is the largest community-built playground of its kind in the world. More than 6,000 volunteers worked on this project.

The Hermitage, home of President Andrew Jackson, is one of many magnificent plantation homes in the Nashville area. Jackson bought the property in 1804.

Andrew Jackson built the Hermitage mansion for his wife Rachel. He and his wife are buried in a tomb in the back of the garden.

The house, with its tall white columns, has been kept in much the same condition as when the Jackson family lived there long ago. There is also a collection of the family's clothing, jewels, and weapons.

East Tennessee

Chattoonaga is for the adventurer. Ride the Incline Railway—the world's steepest passenger railway—up the side of the 2,126-foot (643-m) high Lookout Mountain. Take in the breathtaking natural beauty. At the top, bounce over the swinging bridge to Lover's Leap. On a clear day, you can see seven states. You can also take an elevator to the caverns and the 145-foot (44.2 m) waterfall deep inside the mountain.

At the foot of Lookout Mountain, visit the Tennessee Civil War Museum. Here, you can learn about the important Civil War battles that took place in the Chattanooga area. While you're in the area, visit the Tennessee Aquarium, where more than 9,000 animals fly, swim, and crawl. It is the world's largest freshwater aquarium. The kitchen at the aquarium buys 35,000 crickets, 150 rats, and 300 mice each month to feed the animals.

Ruby Falls is a waterfall inside a limestone cave at Lookout Mountain.

One of the exhibits at the Tennessee Aquarium shows visitors animal life in the Tennessee River.

Next door to the aquarium is the Tennessee Aquarium IMAX 3D Theater. The six-story theater has a screen as long as the eleven anacondas (boa snakes) living in the aquarium's Amazon tank. The projector is the size of a small car. The screen is so large that objects appear to pop out at you.

The Chattanooga African-American Museum/Bessie Smith Hall is located in downtown Chattanooga. The performance hall is dedicated to singer Bessie Smith, America's First Lady of Blues. Exhibits highlight the musical career of Bessie Smith and trace the history of African-Americans living in Chattanooga from 1850 to the present.

About halfway between Chattanooga and Knoxville is Sweetwater, site of the Lost Sea Caverns. The caves are dimly lit to keep them as natural as possible. At one point in the tour, the lights are turned off—leaving visitors wrapped in a blanket of darkness. Visitors can explore the eerie lake in glass-bottom boats. During the hour-long ride across the lake, you can watch as a tour guide feeds mountain trout. Some of these fish weigh more than 20 pounds (10 kg).

Just east of Sweetwater is one of the most popular national parks in the nation—the

Great Smoky Mountains National Park. The park is open year round. Over eight million people visit the park each year for its scenic beauty and outdoor sports.

Just down the road from the Great Smoky Mountains National Park is a small town called Pigeon Forge. It is home to Dollywood. This is singing star Dolly Parton's theme park. Dollywood features craft shops and live entertainment. You can even ride the Tennessee Tornado roller coaster.

Knoxville lies in the shadow of the Great Smoky Mountains, north-west of Pigeon Forge. The mountains and the TVA lakes provide a wide range of activities such as water sports and fishing. Knoxville is the

Many people enjoy the lakes that were created when the TVA built dams in Tennessee.

home of the Tennessee Valley Authority and the University of Tennessee. The University of Tennessee's Lady Vols won six NCAA Division championships in basketball between 1979 and 1998. The football team of the University of Tennessee won a national championship in 1998. The Women's Basketball Hall of Fame is also located in Knoxville.

The state's oldest town, Jonesborough, is a good place to end a tour of Tennessee. The town was founded in 1779. It is on the edge of the Cherokee National Forest in the northeastern part of the state. Chester Inn, the oldest frame building in town, was built before 1800. Many famous people have visited the inn. Tennessee's three Presidents—

The National Storytelling Festival is held during October in Jonesborough. Here, a storyteller holds a crowd spellbound with her ghost story.

Andrew Jackson, James K. Polk, and Andrew Johnson—stayed at the inn at one time or another. Many of the town's homes and churches date back to the mid 1800s. The Jonesborough History Museum offers visitors a step back in time with exhibits from pioneer days. They include a wooden washing machine, cornhusk broom, and quilts.

Tennessee is a beautiful, modern state that preserves and honors its past. There are so many places to see and so many things to do in the Volunteer State that visitors return again and again.

TENNESSEE ALMANAC

Statehood date and number: June 1, 1796, 16th

State seal (date adopted): 1987

State flag (date adopted): 1905

Geographic Center: Rutherford, 5 mi. NE of Murfrees-boro, 36° Lat. N, 86° Long. W

Total area/rank: 42,146 square miles (109,158 sq km)/36th

Borders: Kentucky, Virginia, Georgia, Alabama, Missis-sippi, Arkansas, Missouri, North Carolina

Highest/lowest elevation: Clingman's Dome, 6,643 ft (2,025 m)/Mississippi River, 182 ft (55 m)

Hottest/coldest temperature: 113° F (45° C) at Per-ryville on August 9, 1930/-32° F (-36° C) at Mountain City on December 30, 1917

Land area/rank: 41,219 sq mi (106, 757 sq km)/34th

Population/rank: 5,689,283/16th

Population of major cities:

Memphis: 650,100

Nashville: 545,524

Knoxville: 179,890

Chattanooga: 155,554

Clarksville: 100,455

Johnson City: 55,469

Origin of state name: From *Tanasie*, a Cherokee village

State capital: Nashville

Previous capitals: Knoxville, Nashville, Murfreesboro

Counties: 95

State government: 33 Senators, 99 Representatives

Major rivers, lakes: Mississippi, Tennessee, Cumber-land, Reelfoot Lake

Farm products: Beef cattle, hogs, chickens, horses, dairy products, cotton, soybeans, tobacco, corn, wheat, tomatoes, snap beans, apples, and peaches

Livestock: Cattle, hogs/pigs, chickens

Manufactured products: Paints, medicines, plastics, soap, processed foods, clothing, machinery, electronic and medical equipment, metals, and automobiles

Mining products: Stone, zinc, cement, gravel, clay, coal, and marble

Fishing products: Black bass, carp, perch, catfish, and crappie

Bird: Mockingbird

Dance: Square dance

Flower: Iris

Gem: Tennessee River Pearl

Horse: Tennessee Walking Horse

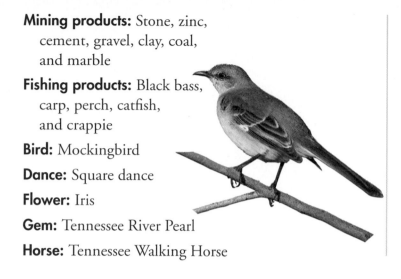

Insects: Firefly and ladybug

Motto: Agriculture and Commerce

Nickname: Volunteer State

Songs: "My Homeland, Tennessee," "When It's Iris Time in Tennessee," "Rocky Top," "My Tennessee," and "Tennessee Waltz"

Stone: Agate

Tree: Tulip poplar

Wild animal: Raccoon

TIME**LINE**

Hernando de Soto seeks gold in the area now known as Tennessee

French and English explore present-day Tennessee

William Bean founds the first white settlement in Tennessee

Tennessee joins Union as sixteenth state

Reelfoot Lake forms after earthquakes strike northwestern Tennessee

Tennessee earns the nickname "Volunteer State" in the war of 1812

The United States forces the Cherokees from their land to Oklahoma

Tennessee is the last state to leave the Union

Tennessee becomes the first state to regain statehood

| 1540 | 1673 | 1769 | 1796 | 1811 | 1812 | 1838 | 1861 | 1866 |

| 1607 | 1620 | 1776 | 1783 | 1787 | 1812–15 | 1843 | 1846–48 | 1861–65 |

The first permanent British settlement at Jamestown, Virginia

Pilgrims set up Plymouth colony

American Revolutionary War ends

U.S. Constitution is written

Pioneers travel West on the Oregon Trail

U.S. fights war with Mexico

American colonies declare independence from England

U.S. and England fight the War of 1812

Civil War occurs in the United States

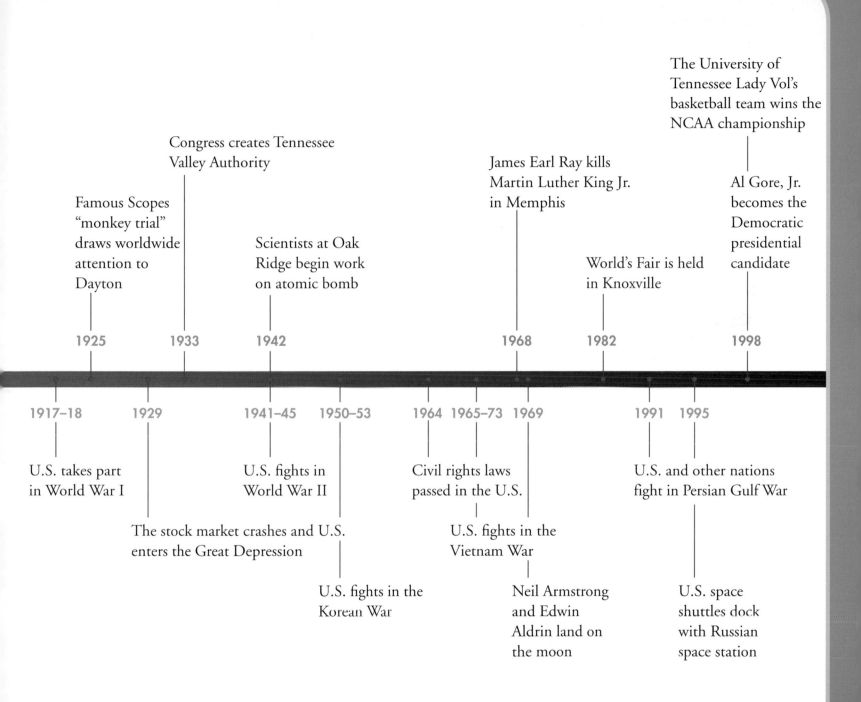

The University of Tennessee Lady Vol's basketball team wins the NCAA championship

Congress creates Tennessee Valley Authority

James Earl Ray kills Martin Luther King Jr. in Memphis

Al Gore, Jr. becomes the Democratic presidential candidate

Famous Scopes "monkey trial" draws worldwide attention to Dayton

Scientists at Oak Ridge begin work on atomic bomb

World's Fair is held in Knoxville

1925   1933   1942   1968   1982   1998

1917–18   1929   1941–45   1950–53   1964 1965–73 1969   1991   1995

U.S. takes part in World War I

U.S. fights in World War II

Civil rights laws passed in the U.S.

U.S. and other nations fight in Persian Gulf War

The stock market crashes and U.S. enters the Great Depression

U.S. fights in the Vietnam War

U.S. fights in the Korean War

Neil Armstrong and Edwin Aldrin land on the moon

U.S. space shuttles dock with Russian space station

GALLERY OF FAMOUS TENNESSEANS

Dorothy Brown
(1919 –)
Surgeon and politician. First African-American woman to be elected to the Tennessee General Assembly.

Albert Gore, Jr.
(1948–)
Vice President under President Bill Clinton. Democratic Presidential candidate in 2000 election.

W.C. Handy
(1873–1958)
Known as the "Father of the Blues." He was born in Alabama, but lived in Memphis. Wrote and published the first blues song in history, "The Memphis Blues."

Cordell Hull
(1871–1955)
U.S. Secretary of State (1933–1944). Born in Overton.

Steve McNair
(1973 –)
Professional football quarterback. Plays for the Tennessee Titans.

Dolly Parton
(1946 –)
Singer, songwriter, and movie star. Born in Locust Ridge.

Elvis Presley
(1935–1977)
Known as "King of Rock and Roll." Lived in Memphis.

Wilma Rudolph
(1940–1994)
Track athlete and winner of three gold medals in the 1960 Olympics. Born in St. Bethlehem.

Margaret Rhea Seddon
(1947 –)
Physician and astronaut on space shuttle *Discovery* in 1985. Born in Murfreesboro.

Bessie Smith
(1894–1937)
Influential blues singer of the 1920s. Born in Chattanooga.

GLOSSARY

ancient: relating to a time early in history

atomic bomb: powerful explosive

bicentennial: a two hundredth anniversary or its celebration

blues: a kind of music expressing sad or unhappy feelings

capital: the city that is the seat of government

capitol: a building in which the government meets

census: a count of the population (every ten years in the United States)

centennial: a hundredth anniversary or its celebration

climate: weather of a region

colony: a group of people living in a new territory but still ruled by the parent country

frontier: a region outside a developed territory

gorge: a narrow steep-walled canyon

impeach: to charge a public official with misconduct

integrate: to give equal opportunities to racial, religious, or ethnic groups

lynch: to put to death by hanging

plantation: a large farm

segregate: to separate according to race, gender, etc.

slave: a person who works without pay and is owned by another person

suffrage: the right to vote

tourism: the business of providing food, housing, and entertainment for visitors

volunteer: someone who offers to do a job without pay

FOR MORE INFORMATION

Web sites

Tennessee Kids' Page

http://www.tn.us/government/kidslink.htm
Tennessee symbols and other historical information.

State of Tennessee

http://www.state.tn.us
The official web site for Tennessee.

Tennessee Department of Tourist Development

http://www.state.tn.us/tourdev
Provides information on sights and travel in Tennessee.

Tennessee Blue Book

http://www.state.tn.us/sos/blue.htm
Provides information of the government of Tennessee.

Books

Aylesworth, Thomas G. and Virginia L. Aylesworth. *The Southeast: Georgia, Kentucky, Tennessee.* New York: Chelsea House Publishers, 1995.

Sanford, William R. and Carl R. Green. *Davy Crockett: Defender of the Alamo.* Berkeley Heights, NJ: Enslow Publishers, 1996.

Thompson, Kathleen. *Tennessee.* Austin: Raintree/Steck-Vaughn Publishers, 1996.

Addresses

Department of Tourist Development
320 6th Avenue, N
Nashville, TN 37202
Promotes Tennessee to vacationers.

Tennessee Historical Commission
2941 Lebanon Road
Nashville, TN 37243
For historical information and cultural landmarks in Tennessee.

Tennessee State Capitol
Nashville, TN 37243-0001
For information on the government of Tennessee.

INDEX

Page numbers in *italics* indicate illustrations

Adair, James, 19
Adelphia Coliseum, 66
African Americans, 26, 30–32, *32*, 34, 39–40, *40*, *41*, *54*, 66
Aluminum Company of America (Alcoa), 36, 56
American Museum of Natural History, 12
ancient, 7, 15
Appalachian Mountains, 5, 7, 10, 19–20
apple crisp recipe, 63
Arthur, Gabriel, 18
atomic bomb, 38, 39, 73, 75
automobile manufacture, 41, *54*, 56, 71

Beale Street, 35–36, 59, *60*
Bean, William, 20, 72
bicentennial, 51, 75
bluegrass music, 52, 62
blues, 35, 52, 59, *60*, 66, 74, 75
breeches, 21
Brooks, Garth, 62
Brooks Museum of Art, 61
Brown, Dorothy, 74
buckskin, 21
Burn, Harry, 34
Byrns, Joseph W., 38

capital, 23, 46–52, 75
capitol, *43*, 46, 48, *49*, 75
Carter family, 35
Carter's Valley, 20
caves, 12
census, 23, 75
centennial, 33, 50, 75
Centennial Exposition, 33
Centennial Park, 50
Charleville, Charles, 18
Chartier, Martin, 19
Chattanooga, *9*, 21, 24, 29, 31, 33, 52, 54, *55*, *58*, 65, 66, 71, 74

Chattanooga African-American Museum/ Bessie Smith Hall, 66
Chattanooga, Battle of, 28
Cherokee, 4, 17, 19–20, 23–25, *25*, 26, *26*, 70, 72
Cherokee language, *26*
Cherokee National Forest, 68
Chester Inn, 68–69
Chickamauga Creek, Battle of, 29, *29*
Chickasaw, 17, 19
civil rights, 39–41, *41*, 61, 73
Civil War, 26–30, *28*, 62, *62*, 72
Clarksville, 72
climate, 12–13, 75
Clinch River, *37*
Clingman, Thomas Lanier, 11, 24
Clingman's Dome, *9*, 10, 11, 24, 70
Coca Cola, 21
colony, 20, 21, 22, 75
Confederacy, 21, 30, 50
Confederate soldiers, 27–29, *29*
Confederate States of America, 27
constitution, state, 23, 43
Constitution, U.S., 30, 31, 34, 40, 72
    amendments, 30, 34
country music, 35, 52, *52*
Country Music Hall of Fame, 49
Crockett, Davy, *24*
Cumberland Gap, *10*
Cumberland Mountain Range, *7*
Cumberland River, 5, 6, 13, *14*, *21*, 46, 49, 66, 71
Cummings, Alexander, 19

dams, 37, 38, *68*
Davis, Sam, 48, 50
Dayton, 35, 75
De Soto, Hernando, 18, *18*, 72
Dollywood, 5, 67
DuPont, 36
Dykeman, Wilma, 68

early exploration, 17–20

earthquakes, 7, 8, 72
Eastman Kodak, 36
East Tennessee region, 8, 10–11, *26*, 27, 33, 52, 56, 65–69
educational system, 42
electricity, development of, 37–38, 53
Emancipation Proclamation, 30
ethnic roots, 53, *53*, *54*
evolution theory, 35, *35*
executive branch, 43–44, *45*

Fall Creek Falls, 11
farming, 17, 26–27, 30–33, 39, 53, 56
  products, 12, 26–27, 36, 57, *58*, 71
Farragut, David, 21, 29
Federal Express Corporation, 57
Fort Donelson, Battle of, 28
Fort Loudon, 19
Fort Nashborough, 46, *49*, 51
fossils, 15
Franklin, 4, 23, 24
Franklin, Battle of, 28
French and Indian War, 19, *19*, 24
French Broad River, 13
Frist, William H., 64
frontier, 21, 75

General Assembly, 44, *44*, *45*, 46
General Motors, 41
geographic regions, 8–12
Gore, Albert, Jr., 42, *42*, 73, 74
gorge, 11, 75
Graceland, 5, 59, 60
Grand Ole Opry, 5, 35, *51*, 62, *62*
Grant, U.S., 28, 29
The Great Depression, 36–38, 73
Great Smokey Mountains, 5, 10, *10*, 25, 67, 68, *68*
  National park, 67

Haley, Alex, *54*
Handy, W.C., 36, 74
Hermitage mansion, *64*, 64–65
Hiwassee River, 17
Holston River, 13
House of Representatives, 44, *44*, *45*, 46, 48

Hull, Cordell, 38, 74

impeach, 75
Indian Removal Act of 1830, 24, 25
Indian Territory, 25
integrate, 39–40, 75

Jackson, Andrew, 23, *24*, 24–25, *25*, 30, 48, *64*, 64–65, 68
Japanese manufacturers, 41–42
Jim Crow Laws, 32, *32*
jobs, 39, *39*, 53, 54–56, 57
Johnson, Andrew, 30, *30*, 47, 68
Johnston, Albert Sidney, 28
Jonesborough, 21, 68, 69
Jonesborough History Museum, 69
judicial branch, *45*, 46
Judicial Selection Commission, 46
Jungle Gym, 64

King, Martin Luther , Jr., 40, *41*, 61, 73
King's Mountain, Battle of, 22, *22*
Kingsport, *13*, 36, 56
Knox, Henry, 24
Knoxville, *9*, 14, 23–24, 31, 41, 52, 54, *55*, *58*, 66, 67, 70, 71, 73
Ku Klux Klan, 31, *31*, 32

LaSalle, René-Robert Cavalier, Sieur de, 18, *18*
legislative branch, 44–46, *45*
Little Tennessee River, 17, 19
Lookout Mountain, 65, *65*
Lost Sea Caverns, 12, 66
Lover's Leap, 65
lynch, 32, *32*, 39, 75
Lynn, Loretta, 62

McKellar, Kenneth D., 38
McNair, Steve, 74
manufacturing, 32–33, 39, 41–42, 53
  products, 54, 56, 71
map of farm/industry products, 58
map of highways, parks and forests, 55
map of Nashville, 49
map of state attractions, 6
map of topography, 9

map of the United States, 2
Marshall, John, 25
Memphis, 9, 18, 24, 31, *32*, 33, 35, 38, 40, 52, *55*, 57, *57*, *58*, 61–62, 71–74
"Memphis Blues," 36, 74
Middle Tennessee, 8, 11–13, 27, 52, 62–65
mining, 33, 56, *58*, 71
Mississippi River, 7–8, *9*, 10, 12–13, 18–20, 57, *57*, 59, 70, 71
Monroe, Bill, 62
Mound Builders, 16, 17
Mountain City, 13, 70
Murfreesboro, *9*, *55*, *58*, 70

Nash, Francis, *21*, 24
Nashborough, 21, *21*, 46
Nashville, *9*, 19, 21, *21*, 24, 31, 33–35, 46–52, *48*, 52, *55*, *58*, 62, 64, 66, 70, 71
Nashville, Battle of, 28
Nashville Toy Museum, 64
National Association for the Advancement of Colored People (NAACP), *32*
National Civil Rights Museum, 61
National Guard, 44
National Storytelling Festival, *69*
Native American, 16–17, 19, 24, *24*, *25*
Needham, James, 18
The 1920's, 35–36
Nolichucky River, 20, *24*
Norris Dam, *37*
North Carolina, 10, 20, 23, *26*
North Holston River, 20

Oak Ridge, 38, *55*, 73
Opryland, 49
Overmountain territories, 21

Parthenon, 33, 49, *50*
Parton, Dolly, 62, 67, 74
Peabody Hotel ducks, 61, *61*
Perryville, 12, 70
Pinnacle Overlook, *10*
Pinson Mounds, *16*, 17
plantations, 26–27, 30, 31, 49, 75

Polk, James Knox, 30, 47, 48, 49, 68
Presley, Elvis, *5*, 59, 74
Proclamation of 1763, 20
Pyramid Arena, 59, *59*

Reconstruction, 30–33
Red Cross, 34
Reelfoot Lake, 7–8, *8*, 62, 71, 72
Revolutionary War, 21, *21*, 23, 24, 72
rivers, 13–14
Robertson, James, *21*
rock and roll, 52, 59, 74
Rockwood Iron Works, *33*
Rodgers, Jimmie, 35
Roosevelt, Franklin D., 37, 38
Roots, Saga of An American Family, 54
Ruby Falls, *65*
Rudolph, Wilma, 74
Ryman Auditorium, *49*, 51, *51*

Scopes, John, 35, *35*
Scopes "Monkey" Trial, 35, 73
secession, 27, 30
Seddon, Margaret Rhea, 74
segregate, 31–32, 75
Senate, 44, *44*, *45*, 48
Sequoya, *24*
service industry, 42
settlers, 19–24, 46
Sevier, John, 22, 23, 47
sharecroppers, 31
Shiloh, Battle of, 28, *28*, 62
Shiloh National Military Park, 62
sit-ins, 39
slave, 26, 27, 30, 75
Smith, Bessie, 36, 66, 74
Smith, Frederick Wallace, 57
statehood, 23–26, 72
Stones River, Battle of, 28
Strickland, William, 46
suffrage, 31–32, 34, 75
Supreme Court, state, *45*, 46

Tanasi, 4, 24, 70
tenant farming, 31
Tennessee, tour of, *57–69*
Tennessee Almanac, 70–71

Tennessee Aquarium, 65, 66, 66
    IMAX 3D theater, 66
Tennessee Bicentennial Capitol Mall, 51
Tennessee Botanical Gardens and Fine
    Arts Center, 49, 51
Tennessee Civil War Museum, 65
Tennessee Equal Suffrage Association, 34
Tennessee River, 9, 12, 13, 17, 37, 41,
    66, 71
Tennessee State Museum, 49, 51, 64
Tennessee Tornado roller coaster, 67
Tennessee Valley Authority (TVA), 37, 37,
    38, 67, 68, 73
Tennessee Walking Horse, 11, 11, 71
timeline, 72–73
Titans football team, 66, 74
Tombigbee Waterway, 41
Trail of Tears, 25, 26
Tritt, Travis, 62
Twentieth Century history, 33–42, 54

Union soldiers, 27, 28, 29, 50
U.S. Army, 33
U.S. Presidents, 30
U.S. Supreme Court, 25, 40
University of Memphis Men's Basketball
    program, 59
University of Tennessee Lady Vol's,
    68, 73

Vanderbilt Transplant Center, 64
Vanderbilt University, 61
volunteer, 4, 7, 28, 57, 69, 72, 79

War of 1812, 4, 23, 24, 29, 72
Watauga Association, 20, 21
Watauga Compact, 20
Watauga River, 20
Wells, Ida B., 32
West Tennessee, 8, 12–13, 27, 52, 57–62
Wildlife Park at Grassmere, 64
Williamson, Alice, 28
Women's Basketball Hall of Fame, 68
World's Fair of 1982, 41, 73
World War I, 33, 34, 34, 36
World War II, 38–39, 39

York, Alvin C., 34, 34, 38

MEET THE AUTHOR

Myra Weatherly grew up in the foothills of South Carolina. As a child, she loved taking trips "over the mountains" to Tennessee. Writing this book has rekindled fond memories of those experiences. Research for the book involved using library resources, surfing the Internet, and talking with Tennesseans.

Myra's published works include books for children and young adults. She holds a master's degree in gifted education. She makes school visits and conducts workshops for parents and teachers.